NO COPYRIG

CW00460526

Kaseke Amalgamated Business Solutions ©

Effective Date: 03/09/2023

This No Copyright Document outlines the terms and conditions related to the courses, videos, books, eBooks, printed books, articles, educational materials, coaching sessions, digital products and print materials owned by Kabsolutions. By accessing, downloading, or using any of our digital products or print materials, you agree to comply with the terms set forth in this document.

Ownership: All digital products and print materials, including but not limited to text, images, graphics, audio, video, and any other content created or produced by Kabsolutions, are the exclusive property of Kabsolutions. All rights, including copyright, are reserved.

Permitted Uses: Personal Use: You may use our digital products and print materials for personal, non-commercial purposes. Commercial Use: For any commercial use or distribution, you must obtain explicit written permission from Kabsolutions. Modification: You may not modify, adapt, or create derivative works based on our digital products or print materials without the express permission of Kabsolutions.

Prohibited Uses: Copyright Violation: You may not reproduce, distribute, display, or perform our digital products or print materials without authorization. Reverse Engineering: You may not reverse engineer, decompile, or disassemble any software or technology associated with our digital products.

Attribution: When using our digital products or print materials, you are not required to provide attribution to Kabsolutions, unless explicitly specified in a separate agreement.

No Warranty: Our digital products and print materials are provided "as is" without any warranty of any kind. Kabsolutions disclaims all warranties, whether expressed or implied, including but not limited to the implied warranties of merchantability and fitness for a particular purpose.

Limitation of Liability: Kabsolutions shall not be liable for any direct, indirect, incidental, special, or consequential damages arising out of or in any way connected with the use of our digital products or print materials.

Changes to Terms: Kabsolutions reserves the right to modify these terms at any time. Any changes will be effective immediately upon posting on our website or other communication channels.

Contact Information: For any questions or requests related to this No Copyright Document, please contact: Kaseke Amalgamated Business Solution ©

Email: contact@kabsolutions.co.uk

Conclusion: By using our digital products or print materials, you acknowledge that you have read, understood, and agreed to the terms and conditions outlined in this No Copyright Document.

Kaseke Amalgamated Business Solutions ®

DISCLAIMER:

Table Of Contents

Chapter 1: Introduction to Business Coaching and Mentoring

The Importance of Business Coaching and Mentoring

In today's fast-paced and competitive business world, the importance of business coaching and mentoring cannot be overstated. Whether you are a start-up, a business owner, or an aspiring entrepreneur, seeking guidance and support from experienced professionals can significantly enhance your chances of success. This subchapter will delve into the invaluable role that business coaching and mentoring play in shaping your entrepreneurial journey and helping you achieve your goals.

First and foremost, business coaching and mentoring provide you with a wealth of knowledge and expertise. Seasoned coaches and mentors have years of experience in various industries and have encountered and overcome numerous challenges. They possess a deep understanding of the intricacies of running a business, from strategic planning to branding, marketing, and financial management. By tapping into their vast knowledge, you can gain insights and perspectives that would otherwise take years to acquire on your own.

Moreover, business coaching and mentoring offer a fresh perspective and objective feedback. As an entrepreneur, it is easy to become immersed in your own ideas and lose sight of potential pitfalls or blind spots. A coach or mentor can provide an unbiased view, helping you identify areas of improvement and offering constructive criticism. Their objective feedback can be a catalyst for growth and development, pushing you to refine your strategies, products, or services.

Furthermore, business coaching and mentoring provide accountability and support. The entrepreneurial journey can be daunting, and it is easy to become overwhelmed or lose focus. A coach or mentor acts as a confidant and sounding board, holding you accountable for your actions and goals. They provide unwavering support, offering guidance and encouragement during challenging times and celebrating your achievements.

Lastly, business coaching and mentoring foster personal and professional growth. A coach or mentor can help you identify and leverage your strengths while addressing areas for improvement. They can guide you in setting realistic goals, developing action plans, and implementing strategies to reach them. Through their guidance, you can enhance your leadership skills, decision-making abilities, and overall business acumen.

In conclusion, business coaching and mentoring are invaluable resources for start-ups, business owners, and entrepreneurs. They provide a wealth of knowledge, offer fresh perspectives, provide accountability and support, and foster personal and professional growth. By seeking the guidance of experienced coaches and mentors, you can navigate the challenges of entrepreneurship with confidence, increasing your chances of achieving your goals and building a successful business.

How Coaching and Mentoring Can Benefit Start-Ups and Business Owners

Start-ups and business owners face numerous challenges as they embark on their entrepreneurial journey. From managing finances to developing effective strategies, the path to success can be demanding and overwhelming. This is where coaching and mentoring play a crucial role in guiding and supporting these individuals to achieve their goals.

Coaching and mentoring offer invaluable support and guidance to start-ups, business owners, and entrepreneurs. They provide a unique opportunity to gain insights from experienced professionals who have already traversed the same path and overcome similar obstacles. The benefits of coaching and mentoring are numerous, and they can significantly impact the success and growth of a business.

Firstly, coaching and mentoring provide an unbiased perspective. When faced with difficult decisions or challenges, it is common for entrepreneurs to become too focused on their own ideas and lose sight of the bigger picture. A coach or mentor can offer an objective viewpoint, helping start-ups and business owners see things from a different angle and make more informed decisions.

Secondly, coaching and mentoring can enhance skills and knowledge. Entrepreneurs often possess a specific skill set that enabled them to start their business, but they may lack expertise in other crucial areas. A coach or mentor can identify these gaps and provide guidance to develop the necessary skills, such as marketing, finance, or leadership. By continuously expanding their knowledge and capabilities, start-ups and business owners can navigate challenges more effectively.

Furthermore, coaching and mentoring can boost confidence and motivation. The entrepreneurial journey can be isolating and filled with self-doubt. Having someone who believes in their potential and provides encouragement can make a significant difference. A coach or mentor can help start-ups and business owners build confidence in their abilities, stay motivated during difficult times, and maintain a positive mindset.

In addition to these benefits, coaching and mentoring also offer networking opportunities. Coaches and mentors often have extensive networks in various industries. By leveraging these connections, start-ups and business owners can gain access to valuable resources, potential partnerships, and even funding opportunities. Networking can open doors that would otherwise remain closed and accelerate the growth of a business.

In conclusion, coaching and mentoring are invaluable resources for start-ups, business owners, and entrepreneurs. The guidance, support, and expertise provided by coaches and mentors can help navigate obstacles, develop new skills, boost confidence, and facilitate networking opportunities. By investing in coaching and mentoring, business owners increase their chances of success and achieve their goals more efficiently.

Chapter 2: Setting Goals for Success

Defining Your Vision and Mission

In the fast-paced and ever-evolving world of business, having a clear vision and mission is essential for the success of any start-up or business venture. Your vision and mission act as guiding principles that drive your actions, decisions, and long-term goals. They serve as a compass, ensuring that you stay focused on your objectives and remain aligned with your core values. This subchapter will delve into the significance of defining your vision and mission and provide invaluable insights on how to craft them effectively.

For start-ups, business owners, and entrepreneurs, having a well-defined vision and mission is the foundation upon which your entire business is built. Your vision statement outlines your aspirations and paints a vivid picture of what you envision your business to become in the future. It encapsulates your dreams, goals, and the impact you aim to create. On the other hand, your mission statement defines the purpose of your business, highlighting the problems you solve and the value you provide to your customers.

Crafting an impactful vision and mission statement requires introspection, strategic thinking, and a deep understanding of your target audience. It involves reflecting on your personal values, your passion for your business, and the unique qualities that set you apart from competitors. Start-ups, business owners, and entrepreneurs must also consider the needs and desires of their target market, ensuring that their vision and mission resonate with their customers.

Business coaching and mentoring play a crucial role in helping individuals define their vision and mission. A skilled coach or mentor can guide entrepreneurs through a process of self-discovery, asking thought-provoking questions that uncover their authentic purpose and goals. They can offer valuable insights and perspectives, helping entrepreneurs gain clarity and refine their vision and mission statements.

By defining your vision and mission, you create a roadmap for success. It becomes easier to set achievable goals, make strategic decisions, and build a strong brand identity. Your vision and mission act as powerful motivators, inspiring you to overcome challenges and persevere in the face of adversity.

In conclusion, defining your vision and mission is a critical step in the entrepreneurial journey. It sets the stage for success and ensures that you remain focused on your objectives. With the guidance of experienced coaches and mentors, start-ups, business owners, and entrepreneurs can craft compelling and authentic vision and mission statements that propel their businesses forward. Embrace the power of a well-defined vision and mission, and watch your entrepreneurial dreams come to life.

Establishing SMART Goals

In the world of entrepreneurship, setting goals is a fundamental step towards success. However, simply having goals is not enough; they need to be SMART goals. This subchapter will delve into the importance of establishing SMART goals and how they can guide start-ups, business owners, and entrepreneurs on their journey towards achieving their aspirations.

SMART is an acronym that stands for Specific, Measurable, Achievable, Relevant, and Time-bound. Each element plays a crucial role in ensuring that goals are well-defined, realistic, and ultimately attainable.

Firstly, goals need to be specific. Vague aspirations such as "increase revenue" or "grow the business" are not sufficient. Start-ups and business owners must clearly outline what they want to achieve, whether it is to increase revenue by a certain percentage, launch a new product, or expand into a new market. By specifying the desired outcome, entrepreneurs can focus their efforts and resources in the right direction.

Furthermore, goals should be measurable. This means setting targets that can be quantified, allowing entrepreneurs to track progress and measure success.

For example, rather than aiming to "improve customer satisfaction," a SMART goal would be to "increase customer satisfaction ratings by 20% within six months." Measurable goals provide a benchmark for evaluating performance and enable entrepreneurs to make necessary adjustments along the way.

Achievability is another crucial aspect of SMART goals. While aiming high is valuable, setting unrealistic goals can hinder progress and demotivate entrepreneurs. Goals should be challenging yet attainable, taking into consideration the available resources, skills, and time frame. By setting achievable goals, entrepreneurs can maintain momentum and boost their confidence as they accomplish each milestone.

Additionally, goals must be relevant to the overall vision and mission of the start-up or business. They should align with the entrepreneur's long-term objectives and contribute to the growth and sustainability of the venture. Setting relevant goals ensures that entrepreneurs are not sidetracked by irrelevant pursuits and remain focused on what truly matters.

Lastly, every goal needs a timeframe. Time-bound goals have a set deadline, creating a sense of urgency and commitment. By assigning a specific date or timeline, entrepreneurs can prioritize their actions and allocate resources effectively. Additionally, time-bound goals provide a framework for planning and allow entrepreneurs to evaluate their progress regularly.

Establishing SMART goals is an essential skill for start-ups, business owners, and entrepreneurs. By following this framework, individuals can set well-defined, measurable, achievable, relevant, and time-bound goals that propel them towards success. Whether it is increasing revenue, expanding market reach, or launching new products, SMART goals provide a roadmap for entrepreneurs in the dynamic and competitive world of business.

In the next chapter, we will explore practical strategies to implement and track SMART goals, helping entrepreneurs stay on track and achieve their desired outcomes.

Creating an Action Plan to Achieve Goals

In the fast-paced world of entrepreneurship, having a clear action plan is crucial for achieving your goals. Without a well-defined roadmap, it is easy to get lost or overwhelmed by the numerous tasks and decisions that come with running a business. This subchapter will guide start-ups, business owners, and entrepreneurs in creating an action plan that will propel their ventures towards success.

1. Define your goals: The first step in creating an action plan is to clearly define your goals. What do you want to achieve in the short-term and long-term? Be specific, measurable, achievable, relevant, and time-bound (SMART) when setting your goals. This will provide you with a clear direction and help you stay focused.

2. Break it down: Once you have defined your goals, break them down into smaller, manageable tasks. Start by identifying the key milestones that need to be achieved to reach your goals. Then, break each milestone into specific tasks. By breaking it down, you can tackle each task systematically and track your progress along the way.

3. Prioritize and set deadlines: Prioritizing tasks is essential to ensure that you are working on the most important and urgent ones first. Evaluate the impact and urgency of each task and assign priorities accordingly. Additionally, set deadlines for each task to create a sense of urgency and accountability.

4. Allocate resources: Determine the resources you need to accomplish your tasks. This includes financial, human, and technological resources. Allocate resources efficiently and consider outsourcing certain tasks if necessary. By ensuring you have the right resources in place, you can work more effectively towards your goals.

5. Monitor and adjust: Regularly monitor your progress and make adjustments when needed. Assess whether you are on track to achieving your goals and

make necessary changes to your action plan. This will help you stay adaptable and responsive to the ever-changing business landscape.

6. Seek support and accountability: Surround yourself with a network of mentors, coaches, or fellow entrepreneurs who can provide guidance and support. Share your action plan with them and seek their feedback. They can hold you accountable and provide valuable insights to help you overcome challenges and stay motivated.

By creating an action plan to achieve your goals, you are setting yourself up for success as an entrepreneur. Remember, a well-defined plan is not set in stone, but rather a guide that can be adjusted as you navigate the entrepreneurial journey. Stay committed, stay resilient, and most importantly, stay focused on achieving your goals.

Chapter 3: Developing a Strong Mindset

Overcoming Self-Limiting Beliefs

In the journey to success, one of the greatest obstacles that entrepreneurs face is their own self-limiting beliefs. These beliefs can hold us back from taking risks, pursuing our dreams, and achieving our goals. However, with the right mindset and strategies, it is possible to overcome these self-imposed limitations and unlock our full potential.

In this subchapter, we will explore the common self-limiting beliefs that entrepreneurs often encounter and provide practical techniques to overcome them. By addressing these beliefs head-on, we can break free from the constraints that hold us back and pave the way for personal and professional growth.

One of the most common self-limiting beliefs is the fear of failure. Many entrepreneurs hesitate to take risks because they are afraid of making mistakes or facing setbacks. However, it is important to reframe failure as a learning opportunity rather than a measure of personal worth. Embracing a growth mindset allows us to view failure as a stepping stone towards success, enabling us to learn from our experiences and make better decisions in the future.

Another self-limiting belief that entrepreneurs often grapple with is the imposter syndrome. This belief convinces us that we are not qualified or deserving of success, despite evidence to the contrary. Overcoming imposter syndrome involves recognizing our achievements, acknowledging our skills and expertise, and seeking support from mentors or business coaches who can provide objective perspectives.

Furthermore, the belief that success is reserved for others or that there is a limited amount of success available can also hinder our progress. This scarcity mentality can lead to self-sabotaging behaviors and prevent us from taking advantage of opportunities. By shifting our mindset to one of abundance, we can embrace collaboration, networking, and strategic partnerships, realizing that there is enough success to go around for everyone.

To overcome self-limiting beliefs, it is crucial to practice self-awareness and challenge our negative thoughts. By questioning the validity of these beliefs and replacing them with empowering affirmations, we can reshape our mindset and build confidence in our abilities.

In conclusion, overcoming self-limiting beliefs is a crucial step towards achieving our goals as entrepreneurs. By recognizing and challenging these beliefs, reframing failure, embracing our achievements, adopting an abundance mindset, and practicing self-awareness, we can break free from our constraints and unlock our full potential. As we embark on this journey of personal and professional growth, let us remember that the only limits that truly exist are the ones we impose upon ourselves.

Cultivating a Growth Mindset

In the dynamic and challenging world of entrepreneurship, having a growth mindset is crucial for achieving long-term success. This subchapter explores the concept of cultivating a growth mindset, and how it can empower start-ups, business owners, and entrepreneurs to overcome obstacles and achieve their goals.

A growth mindset is the belief that intelligence and abilities can be developed through dedication, hard work, and a commitment to learning. Unlike a fixed mindset, which assumes that abilities are innate and unchangeable, a growth mindset embraces challenges and sees failures as opportunities for growth.

For start-ups, business owners, and entrepreneurs, cultivating a growth mindset is essential for navigating the ever-evolving business landscape. By adopting a growth mindset, individuals can embrace innovation, adapt to change, and continuously improve their skills and knowledge. This mindset allows them to view setbacks and failures as valuable learning experiences, rather than insurmountable obstacles.

To cultivate a growth mindset, it is important to start by fostering a passion for learning and personal development. Start-ups and business owners should actively seek out opportunities to expand their knowledge and acquire new skills. This can be achieved through attending industry conferences, participating in workshops, or enrolling in business coaching and mentoring programs.

Additionally, surrounding oneself with a supportive network of like-minded individuals can also contribute to the growth mindset journey. By engaging in conversations with fellow entrepreneurs, sharing experiences, and seeking advice, start-ups and business owners can gain valuable insights and perspectives that can help them overcome challenges and achieve their goals.

Furthermore, it is crucial to embrace failure as a stepping stone to success. Start-ups and business owners should view failures as valuable feedback and use them as opportunities for learning and growth. By analyzing mistakes, identifying areas for improvement, and making necessary adjustments, entrepreneurs can refine their strategies and approaches, ultimately leading to greater success in the long run.

In conclusion, cultivating a growth mindset is a critical component of entrepreneurial success. By fostering a passion for learning, surrounding oneself with supportive individuals, and embracing failure as an opportunity for growth, start-ups, business owners, and entrepreneurs can navigate the ever-changing business landscape with resilience and determination. By adopting a growth mindset, individuals can unlock their full potential, achieve their goals, and create lasting success for their businesses.

Building Resilience and Persistence

In the fast-paced and competitive world of entrepreneurship, building resilience and persistence is essential for success. The ability to bounce back from setbacks, adapt to challenges, and stay motivated in the face of adversity can make all the difference between failure and achieving your goals. This subchapter will explore strategies and techniques to help start-ups, business owners, and entrepreneurs develop resilience and persistence on their entrepreneurial journey.

Resilience is the ability to withstand and recover from difficult situations. It is about maintaining a positive mindset, even when faced with obstacles and failures. One way to build resilience is by cultivating a growth mindset. Embracing the belief that failures and setbacks are opportunities for learning and growth can help entrepreneurs bounce back stronger. By reframing challenges as stepping stones to success, entrepreneurs can develop the mental toughness needed to persevere.

Another key aspect of resilience is self-care. Entrepreneurs often pour all their time and energy into their businesses, neglecting their own well-being. However, neglecting self-care can lead to burnout and decreased resilience. It is crucial for entrepreneurs to prioritize their physical and mental health through regular exercise, healthy eating, and engaging in activities that bring joy and relaxation.

Persistence is the ability to stay focused and committed to achieving long-term goals, even in the face of obstacles and setbacks. Entrepreneurs must develop the mindset of not giving up easily and consistently work towards their vision. One effective strategy for building persistence is setting realistic and achievable goals. Breaking down larger goals into smaller milestones not only provides a sense of accomplishment but also keeps entrepreneurs motivated and focused.

Building a strong support network is another crucial factor in developing persistence. Surrounding oneself with like-minded individuals who understand the challenges of entrepreneurship can provide valuable support and encouragement. Joining business coaching and mentoring programs can offer guidance, accountability, and a network of peers who can relate to the entrepreneurial journey.

In conclusion, building resilience and persistence is essential for start-ups, business owners, and entrepreneurs to navigate the challenges of entrepreneurship successfully. By cultivating a growth mindset, prioritizing self-care, setting achievable goals, and building a strong support network, entrepreneurs can develop the mental toughness and determination needed to overcome obstacles and achieve their goals. Remember, resilience and persistence are not innate qualities but skills that can be developed with practice and determination.

Chapter 4: Building a Solid Foundation

Understanding Business Structures and Legalities

Starting a business is an exhilarating journey that requires careful planning, strategic thinking, and a thorough understanding of business structures and legalities. In this subchapter, we will delve into the essentials of business structures and the legal aspects that every start-up, business owner, and entrepreneur must be aware of. Whether you are just starting out or looking to expand your existing business, this information will provide you with valuable insights to navigate the complex world of entrepreneurship.

First and foremost, selecting the right business structure is crucial as it determines the legal and financial obligations of your venture. We will explore the various options, such as sole proprietorship, partnership, limited liability company (LLC), and corporation, highlighting the advantages and disadvantages of each. Understanding the implications of these structures will help you make an informed decision based on your goals, risk tolerance, and growth plans.

Moreover, legalities play a pivotal role in safeguarding your business and ensuring compliance with the law. From obtaining the necessary permits and licenses to protecting your intellectual property, we will guide you through the maze of legal requirements. We will discuss the importance of contracts, including employment agreements, vendor contracts, and customer agreements, and provide insights on how to draft and negotiate them to protect your interests.

As a start-up or business owner, it is vital to understand the tax obligations associated with your business structure. We will provide an overview of tax considerations, such as income tax, sales tax, and employment tax, and offer guidance on how to navigate the complex tax landscape while maximizing deductions and minimizing liabilities.

Furthermore, we will address the importance of maintaining proper records and financial documentation. Sound financial management is crucial for the success and growth of any business. We will discuss the basics of bookkeeping, financial statements, and the importance of budgeting and forecasting. Understanding these concepts will empower you to make informed financial decisions and attract potential investors or lenders.

In conclusion, understanding business structures and legalities is fundamental for any start-up, business owner, or entrepreneur. By equipping yourself with this knowledge, you will not only protect your business but also ensure its long-term success. Remember, seeking professional advice from business coaches and mentors can provide invaluable guidance throughout your entrepreneurial journey. So, let's dive into the intricacies of business structures and legalities and pave the way for a prosperous and fulfilling entrepreneurial venture.

Conducting Market Research

Market research is an essential component of any successful business strategy. It provides valuable insights into customer needs and preferences, helps identify potential opportunities and threats, and guides decision-making processes. As an entrepreneur, conducting thorough market research can significantly contribute to the growth and sustainability of your business.

Understanding your target market is crucial for any business. By conducting market research, you can gain a deep understanding of your customers' demographics, psychographics, and buying behavior. This information allows you to tailor your products or services to meet their specific needs, thereby increasing customer satisfaction and loyalty.

One of the primary goals of market research is to identify your competitors and analyze their strengths and weaknesses. By understanding your competition, you can differentiate yourself and develop a unique selling proposition that sets you apart. This knowledge helps you position your brand effectively and create marketing strategies that attract and retain customers.

Market research also helps you identify emerging trends and potential market opportunities. By staying informed about industry developments, customer preferences, and technological advancements, you can adapt your business to meet changing market demands. This flexibility is crucial for startups and business owners who need to stay ahead of the curve and remain competitive in their respective niches.

There are various methods to conduct market research, including surveys, focus groups, interviews, and online research. Each method has its advantages and disadvantages, and the choice depends on your specific needs and resources. Utilizing a combination of these methods can provide a comprehensive understanding of your market and facilitate informed decision-making.

In conclusion, market research is an invaluable tool for startups, business owners, and entrepreneurs in the business coaching and mentoring industry. By conducting thorough market research, you can gain insights into your target market, identify competitors, spot emerging trends, and capitalize on market opportunities. Remember, conducting market research is an ongoing process, as market dynamics and consumer preferences are constantly evolving. By continuously gathering and analyzing data, you can ensure the long-term success of your business and achieve your entrepreneurial goals.

Defining Your Target Audience

One of the key factors in the success of any business is understanding and defining your target audience. Whether you are a start-up, business owner, or entrepreneur, knowing who your customers are and how to reach them is essential for achieving your goals. This subchapter will guide you through the process of defining your target audience, helping you focus your efforts and resources effectively.

In the world of business coaching and mentoring, understanding your target audience becomes even more crucial. As a coach or mentor, you need to identify the specific group of individuals who can benefit the most from your expertise. Defining your target audience allows you to tailor your services and messaging to meet their unique needs and challenges.

To begin, take a step back and analyze your current customer base. Who are your most loyal and profitable customers? What characteristics do they share? Are they individuals or businesses? What industries do they belong to? By answering these questions, you can start building a profile of your ideal customer.

Next, consider conducting market research to gain deeper insights into your target audience. This research can include surveys, interviews, and analysis of industry reports. Look for patterns and trends that can help you identify the common pain points, goals, and desires shared by your target audience. This information will allow you to tailor your products, services, and marketing efforts to address their specific needs effectively.

Another useful tool in defining your target audience is creating buyer personas. A buyer persona is a fictional representation of your ideal customer, including demographics, interests, motivations, and challenges. By developing well-rounded personas, you can better understand the behaviors and preferences of your target audience, enabling you to align your messaging and marketing strategies accordingly.

Once you have defined your target audience, it is essential to continuously monitor and reassess your understanding of them. Markets evolve, and customer needs change over time. Stay up-to-date with industry trends, engage with your customers regularly, and be open to feedback. This ongoing process of refining your understanding of your target audience will ensure that your business remains relevant and successful in the long run.

In conclusion, defining your target audience is a critical step for start-ups, business owners, and entrepreneurs in the field of business coaching and mentoring. By knowing who your customers are and what they need, you can tailor your services and marketing efforts to effectively reach and serve them. Continuously monitor and reassess your understanding of your target audience to stay ahead of the curve and position your business for success.

Chapter 5: Crafting a Winning Business Plan

The Purpose and Components of a Business Plan

As an aspiring entrepreneur, starting a new business venture can be an exhilarating yet challenging journey. To ensure success in this competitive landscape, it is crucial to have a well-thought-out business plan. This subchapter will walk you through the purpose and components of a business plan, providing you with a roadmap to achieve your entrepreneurial goals.

The purpose of a business plan is to serve as a comprehensive blueprint for your business. It outlines your vision, mission, and objectives, helping you establish a clear roadmap towards success. Whether you are a start-up or an established business owner, a business plan acts as a guiding document that keeps you focused and accountable.

There are several key components that make up a well-rounded business plan. First and foremost, an executive summary provides a concise overview of your business, highlighting its unique selling proposition and competitive advantage. This section grabs the attention of potential investors or partners and sets the tone for the rest of the plan.

Next, a detailed company description delves into the core aspects of your business. It includes information about your industry, target market, and competitive analysis. This section showcases your understanding of the market and your ability to position your business effectively.

Furthermore, a comprehensive marketing and sales strategy outlines how you plan to attract and retain customers. This includes market research, pricing strategies, distribution channels, and promotional activities. A strong marketing and sales plan demonstrates your ability to reach your target audience and generate revenue.

Financial projections and analysis are also critical components of a business plan. These sections provide an overview of your company's financial health, including revenue forecasts, budgeting, and cash flow management. Investors and lenders will closely scrutinize these numbers to evaluate the viability and profitability of your business.

Lastly, a well-developed business plan includes an operational plan that outlines your day-to-day operations, staffing needs, and any legal or regulatory requirements. This section demonstrates your ability to effectively manage and scale your business.

In conclusion, a business plan is an essential tool for start-ups, business owners, and entrepreneurs. It provides a roadmap for success and acts as a comprehensive blueprint for your business. By including key elements such as an executive summary, company description, marketing and sales strategy, financial projections, and operational plan, you can ensure that your business plan is well-rounded and compelling. With a solid business plan in hand, you will be well-prepared to navigate the challenges and opportunities of the entrepreneurial journey.

Conducting a SWOT Analysis

In the world of business, one of the most effective tools for evaluating your company's strengths, weaknesses, opportunities, and threats is the SWOT analysis. This powerful technique provides valuable insights into the internal and external factors that can impact your business's success. Whether you are a start-up, business owner, or entrepreneur, conducting a SWOT analysis is an essential step towards achieving your goals.

Strengths refer to the internal attributes and resources that set your business apart from the competition. These could include things like a unique product or service, a talented team, strong brand recognition, or efficient processes. Identifying and leveraging your strengths is crucial for building a competitive advantage and positioning your business for success.

Weaknesses, on the other hand, are the areas where your business falls short or faces challenges. It could be a lack of financial resources, inadequate marketing strategies, or a shortage of skilled staff. Recognizing your weaknesses allows you to develop strategies for improvement and minimize potential risks.

Opportunities are external factors that have the potential to positively impact your business. These could be emerging market trends, new customer segments, technological advancements, or changes in regulations. By identifying opportunities, you can capitalize on them and drive growth for your business.

Threats are external factors that can potentially harm your business. These may include intense competition, economic downturns, changing consumer preferences, or legal and regulatory challenges. Understanding the threats helps you develop contingency plans and mitigate risks.

To conduct a SWOT analysis, begin by gathering data from various sources such as customer feedback, market research, and competitor analysis. Then, organize this information into four quadrants—Strengths, Weaknesses, Opportunities, and Threats—using a visual representation like a table or a graph.

The next step involves analyzing each quadrant and identifying key insights. This process will help you understand how your strengths can be leveraged, weaknesses can be addressed, opportunities can be seized, and threats can be minimized. The insights gained from a SWOT analysis can inform your strategic planning, marketing efforts, resource allocation, and decision-making processes.

Remember that a SWOT analysis is not a one-time exercise but an ongoing process. As your business evolves and the market landscape changes, it is essential to regularly revisit and update your analysis to stay ahead of the curve.

By conducting a SWOT analysis, you will gain a deeper understanding of your business's position in the market and uncover new opportunities for growth. It will serve as a compass, guiding your strategic decisions and helping you navigate the challenges that come your way. So, take the time to conduct a thorough SWOT analysis and equip yourself with the knowledge to drive your business towards success.

Developing a Marketing and Sales Strategy

In today's competitive business landscape, developing a robust marketing and sales strategy is crucial for start-ups, business owners, and entrepreneurs. This subchapter will guide you through the process of creating an effective plan that will help you achieve your goals and propel your business forward.

A well-crafted marketing and sales strategy not only helps you attract potential customers but also ensures that you convert leads into loyal clients. It is the backbone of your business growth and lays the foundation for long-term success. Let's dive into the key steps involved in developing this strategy.

1. Define Your Target Market: Understanding your target market is the first step towards developing a successful marketing and sales strategy. Identify who your ideal customers are, their needs, preferences, and pain points. This knowledge will help you tailor your messaging and reach the right audience.

2. Conduct Market Research: Thorough market research is essential to gain insights into your industry, competitors, and trends. Analyze your competitors' strategies, pricing, and target audience to identify gaps and opportunities. This knowledge will enable you to position your product or service effectively in the market.

3. Set Clear Marketing Objectives: Define your marketing objectives based on your business goals. Whether it's increasing brand awareness, generating leads, or driving sales, make sure your objectives are specific, measurable, attainable, relevant, and time-bound (SMART).

4. Develop a Branding Strategy: Your brand is more than just a logo; it represents your company's personality and values. Develop a strong brand identity that resonates with your target audience. Craft a compelling brand story and ensure consistency across all marketing channels.

5. Create a Content Marketing Plan: Content marketing plays a crucial role in establishing your authority and building trust with your audience. Develop a content marketing plan that includes creating valuable and relevant content, such as blog posts, videos, social media posts, and podcasts. Consistently deliver content that addresses your customers' pain points and educates them about your solutions.

6. Implement Sales Strategies: Design a sales strategy that aligns with your marketing efforts. Train your sales team to effectively communicate your value proposition, handle objections, and close deals. Utilize sales tools and technology to streamline the sales process and track performance.

7. Measure and Analyze Results: Set up key performance indicators (KPIs) to measure the success of your marketing and sales efforts. Regularly analyze data and metrics to identify areas for improvement and make data-driven decisions.

By following these steps and continuously adapting your strategy based on market changes, you will establish a solid foundation for your business's marketing and sales success. Remember, developing a marketing and sales strategy is an ongoing process, and it requires constant evaluation and refinement to stay ahead in today's competitive business world.

Chapter 6: Effective Communication and Leadership

Enhancing Interpersonal Skills

In the fast-paced and ever-evolving world of entrepreneurship, the ability to effectively communicate and build strong relationships is paramount to success. As a start-up, business owner, or entrepreneur, the importance of enhancing your interpersonal skills cannot be emphasized enough. This subchapter aims to guide you on a journey of self-improvement, helping you develop the necessary skills to navigate the complex web of business relationships and achieve your goals.

1. Active Listening: Active listening is the foundation of effective communication. By attentively listening to your team members, clients, and partners, you will gain valuable insights and foster a sense of trust and respect. This skill allows you to understand the needs and concerns of others, enabling you to provide tailored solutions and build stronger connections.

2. Emotional Intelligence: Being aware of your own emotions and those of others is vital in business interactions. Emotional intelligence helps you handle conflicts, manage stress, and build positive relationships. By understanding and empathizing with others, you can create a harmonious work environment, resolve disputes amicably, and inspire your team to achieve greatness.

3. Non-Verbal Communication: Communication extends beyond words. Your body language, facial expressions, and tone of voice can convey powerful messages. Mastering non-verbal communication can help you establish rapport, convey confidence, and create a positive impression. Paying attention to your own non-verbal cues and interpreting others' will improve your ability to connect and influence others effectively.

4. Conflict Resolution: In any business, conflicts are bound to arise. Developing conflict resolution skills is essential to maintain healthy relationships and minimize disruptions. By adopting a collaborative approach, actively listening to all parties involved, and seeking win-win solutions, you can transform conflicts into opportunities for growth and innovation.

5. Networking and Relationship Building: Building a strong network is crucial in the world of entrepreneurship. Cultivating genuine relationships with potential clients, mentors, and industry peers can open doors to new opportunities and collaborations. Attend industry events, join professional organizations, and leverage social media platforms to expand your network and create lasting connections.

By enhancing your interpersonal skills, you will not only improve your own personal and professional growth but also create a positive and supportive work environment. As you navigate the challenging path of entrepreneurship, remember that success is not achieved alone but through the power of strong relationships and effective communication. Invest in developing your interpersonal skills, and you will reap the rewards of enhanced collaboration, increased productivity, and sustainable growth.

Building Effective Teams

In the fast-paced world of business, success is often dependent on the strength and cohesion of a team. Whether you are a start-up founder or a seasoned business owner, understanding how to build and maintain effective teams is critical to achieving your goals. This subchapter will guide you through the process of creating a high-performing team that can propel your business to new heights.

1. Defining Roles and Responsibilities: To build an effective team, it is essential to clearly define the roles and responsibilities of each team member. This ensures that everyone understands their individual contributions and how they fit into the bigger picture. By clarifying expectations and setting

achievable goals, you can foster a sense of accountability and motivation within the team.

2. Diversity and Complementary Skills: A successful team comprises individuals with diverse backgrounds, skills, and perspectives. Embracing diversity not only enhances creativity and innovation but also expands your business's reach and customer base. Seek team members who possess complementary skills, as this can lead to increased productivity and efficiency.

3. Communication and Collaboration: Effective communication is the cornerstone of any successful team. Encourage open and transparent communication channels, both within the team and with external stakeholders. Foster a collaborative environment where team members feel comfortable sharing ideas, asking questions, and providing feedback. Regular team meetings and brainstorming sessions can help foster a sense of unity and facilitate the exchange of ideas.

4. Building Trust and Resolving Conflict: Trust is a crucial element in team dynamics. Encourage trust-building activities and foster an environment where team members feel safe to express themselves without fear of judgment or reprisal. Conflict is inevitable in any team setting, but it is how it is managed that determines its impact. Teach conflict resolution strategies and encourage open dialogue to resolve conflicts constructively.

5. Continuous Learning and Development: Encourage a culture of continuous learning and development within your team. Provide opportunities for professional growth through training, workshops, and mentoring programs. By investing in your team's development, you not only enhance their skills and knowledge but also foster loyalty and commitment.

Building an effective team is an ongoing process that requires time, effort, and commitment. However, the rewards are immense. A high-performing team can drive innovation, boost productivity, and help you achieve your business goals. By following the principles outlined in this subchapter, you can build a team that is capable of navigating the challenges of entrepreneurship and propelling your business towards success.

Leading with Purpose and Integrity

Subchapter: Leading with Purpose and Integrity

Introduction:
In the journey of entrepreneurship, one of the most crucial elements that sets successful businesses apart is the ability to lead with purpose and integrity. This subchapter delves into the significance of these qualities and offers practical insights to help start-ups, business owners, and entrepreneurs cultivate a leadership style that creates a positive impact. By embracing purpose and integrity, individuals can steer their companies towards sustainable growth and long-term success.

1. Defining Purposeful Leadership:
Leading with purpose entails aligning your actions, decisions, and goals with the core values and mission of your business. It involves understanding the bigger picture and inspiring others to work towards a common vision. This section explores the importance of purposeful leadership and provides strategies for discovering and articulating your organization's purpose.

2. The Role of Integrity in Leadership:
Integrity is the foundation upon which ethical leadership is built. This section emphasizes the significance of integrity in business and the positive impact it has on employee morale, customer trust, and overall company reputation. It offers practical tips on how to cultivate integrity within your leadership style and create a culture of transparency and honesty.

3. Ethical Decision-Making:
Ethical decision-making is a critical skill that every leader must possess. This part of the subchapter highlights the challenges entrepreneurs often face when making tough choices and provides a framework for making ethical decisions.

It also addresses common ethical dilemmas in business and offers guidance on how to navigate them while upholding integrity.

4. Building a Purpose-driven Culture:
Creating a purpose-driven culture is essential for attracting and retaining top talent, fostering innovation, and driving business growth. This section explores strategies for instilling purpose within your organization and empowering employees to connect their work with a greater sense of meaning and fulfillment.

5. Leading by Example:
Leadership by example is a powerful tool for inspiring and motivating others. This final section emphasizes the importance of consistency between your words and actions, and offers guidance on how to lead by example in various aspects of your business, including communication, teamwork, and ethical conduct.

Conclusion:
Leading with purpose and integrity is not only a moral imperative but also a strategic advantage for start-ups, business owners, and entrepreneurs. By embracing these qualities, you can build a strong foundation for your business, attract loyal customers, and create a positive impact on society. This subchapter equips you with practical insights and strategies to become a purpose-driven leader who inspires others and achieves long-term success.

Chapter 7: Financial Management and Funding

Financial Planning and Budgeting

As an entrepreneur, one of the most vital aspects of running a successful business is financial planning and budgeting. In this subchapter, we will explore the significance of effective financial management and provide practical tips on creating a solid financial plan for start-ups and established businesses alike.

Financial planning serves as the foundation for your business's financial success. It involves setting financial goals, forecasting revenues and expenses, and developing strategies to achieve those goals. By creating a comprehensive financial plan, you can identify potential risks and opportunities, make informed decisions, and stay on track towards your business objectives.

Budgeting, on the other hand, is a critical tool that helps you manage your cash flow effectively. It involves allocating resources based on your financial plan and tracking your income and expenses. A well-designed budget allows you to monitor your business's financial health, make necessary adjustments, and ensure that you have enough funds for essential operations and growth.

For start-ups, financial planning and budgeting may seem overwhelming, but it's crucial to establish these practices early on. By creating a realistic financial plan and budget, you can secure funding, attract investors, and demonstrate your commitment to financial stability. Additionally, it enables you to assess the feasibility of your business idea and identify potential pitfalls before they become major challenges.

For established businesses, financial planning and budgeting play an equally significant role. They provide a roadmap for growth, help you manage cash flow during expansion or downturns, and ensure that you are making the most of your resources. By regularly reviewing and adjusting your financial plan and budget, you can adapt to market changes, optimize your resources, and stay ahead of your competition.

In this subchapter, we will guide you through the process of financial planning and budgeting, offering valuable insights and practical advice. We will cover topics such as setting financial goals, conducting market research, forecasting revenues and expenses, managing cash flow, and monitoring financial performance. Additionally, we will share tips on leveraging financial tools and technologies to streamline your financial processes and make informed decisions.

Whether you are just starting your entrepreneurial journey or have been in business for years, mastering financial planning and budgeting is essential for long-term success. By implementing effective practices and leveraging the right tools, you can navigate financial challenges, seize growth opportunities, and achieve your business goals.

Understanding Cash Flow

Cash flow is one of the most critical aspects of running a successful business. In this subchapter, we will delve into the importance of understanding cash flow and how it can impact the growth and sustainability of your start-up or business. Whether you are a seasoned business owner or an aspiring entrepreneur, mastering cash flow management is essential for achieving your goals.

Cash flow refers to the movement of money in and out of your business. It is not just about revenue or sales; it encompasses all the financial activities that affect your available cash. Understanding your cash flow helps you make informed decisions, plan for the future, and avoid potential pitfalls that could cripple your business.

For start-ups, careful management of cash flow is even more critical. Many new businesses fail due to insufficient cash flow, even if they have a great product or service. By understanding and monitoring your cash flow, you can identify potential cash shortages early on and take proactive measures to mitigate them.

In this subchapter, we will explore various aspects of cash flow management, including:

1. Cash Flow Statement: We will guide you through creating a cash flow statement, which provides a detailed breakdown of your cash inflows and outflows. This statement is a valuable tool for assessing the health of your business and identifying areas that require attention.

2. Cash Flow Forecasting: We will discuss the importance of cash flow forecasting and how it helps you anticipate future cash needs. By accurately projecting your cash flow, you can plan for expansion, manage seasonal fluctuations, and make informed decisions about investments and expenses.

3. Cash Flow Strategies: We will provide practical tips and strategies for improving your cash flow. From optimizing your receivables and payables to exploring financing options, you will learn how to effectively manage your cash flow and maintain a healthy financial position.

4. Cash Flow Troubleshooting: We will address common cash flow issues faced by start-ups and business owners and provide solutions to overcome them. By understanding the warning signs and implementing corrective measures, you can navigate through cash flow challenges and ensure the long-term success of your business.

Understanding cash flow is vital for all entrepreneurs and business owners. By mastering the principles and techniques outlined in this subchapter, you will be equipped with the knowledge and skills to make informed financial decisions and drive your business towards success.

Exploring Funding Options for Start-Ups

When it comes to starting a new venture, one of the biggest challenges entrepreneurs face is securing funding. Without adequate capital, even the most brilliant ideas can struggle to take off. In this subchapter, we will explore various funding options available to start-ups, providing valuable insights to help you navigate the complex landscape of financing your business.

1. Bootstrapping: Many successful entrepreneurs have started their businesses by self-funding or bootstrapping. This involves using personal savings, credit cards, or borrowing from friends and family to cover initial expenses. While it may require sacrifices and a lean approach, bootstrapping allows you to retain full control of your company and avoid the pressure of debt.

2. Angel Investors: Angel investors are affluent individuals who provide capital to start-ups in exchange for equity or convertible debt. These experienced entrepreneurs often bring valuable industry knowledge and networks to the table, making them ideal mentors for early-stage businesses.

3. Venture Capital: Venture capitalists are firms that invest in start-ups with high growth potential. In addition to providing capital, they often offer strategic guidance and industry contacts. However, securing venture capital can be highly competitive, as investors typically seek businesses with strong growth prospects and a solid business plan.

4. Crowdfunding: Crowdfunding platforms have gained popularity in recent years, allowing entrepreneurs to raise funds from a large number of individuals. By leveraging social media and online networks, start-ups can showcase their ideas and attract supporters who contribute small amounts of money. Crowdfunding not only provides capital but also serves as a marketing tool, generating buzz and awareness for your business.

5. Small Business Administration (SBA) Loans: The SBA offers loans with favorable terms to small businesses. These loans can be used for a wide range

of business needs, including working capital, equipment purchase, and real estate investment. SBA loans often have lower interest rates and longer repayment terms, making them an attractive option for start-ups.

6. Incubators and Accelerators: Start-up incubators and accelerators provide a supportive environment for entrepreneurs, offering mentorship, resources, and sometimes funding. These programs typically involve a structured curriculum and networking opportunities, helping start-ups refine their business models and attract investors.

7. Grants and Competitions: Many organizations and government agencies offer grants and competitions specifically designed to support innovative start-ups. These funding opportunities often come with additional benefits, such as mentorship, access to resources, and exposure to potential investors.

As an entrepreneur or business owner, understanding the funding options available to you is crucial for turning your visions into reality. By carefully considering these options and tailoring your approach to your specific needs, you can secure the financial backing necessary to bring your start-up to life.

Chapter 8: Marketing and Branding Strategies

Building a Strong Brand Identity

In the competitive landscape of today's business world, a strong brand identity is crucial for the success and longevity of any start-up or business. It is the foundation upon which all marketing efforts are built and the key to establishing a lasting connection with customers. In this subchapter, we will delve into the importance of building a strong brand identity and provide practical strategies for start-ups, business owners, and entrepreneurs to create a brand that resonates with their target audience.

First and foremost, it is essential to understand what brand identity entails. It goes beyond a catchy logo or a memorable tagline. A brand identity encompasses the core values, mission, and personality of a business. It is the unique way in which a company communicates its offerings, values, and promises to its customers. By crafting a compelling brand identity, start-ups and business owners can differentiate themselves from their competitors and foster trust and loyalty among their target audience.

One of the first steps towards building a strong brand identity is conducting thorough market research. Understanding the needs, desires, and pain points of your target audience will enable you to tailor your brand messaging and visual elements to resonate with them. By identifying your target market's preferences and values, you can create a brand identity that appeals directly to their emotions and aspirations.

Consistency is another key aspect of a strong brand identity. Start-ups and business owners must ensure that their brand messaging, visual elements, and customer experience remain consistent across all touchpoints. This consistency helps in building recognition and trust among customers, as they become familiar with your brand and its unique qualities.

Furthermore, a strong brand identity should be reflected in every aspect of a business, from its website design and packaging to its customer service. Every interaction a customer has with your business should align with the values and personality of your brand. By delivering a consistent and cohesive brand experience, start-ups and business owners can create a strong brand identity that resonates with their target audience and sets them apart from their competitors.

In conclusion, building a strong brand identity is vital for the success of start-ups, business owners, and entrepreneurs. By conducting thorough market research, establishing consistency, and reflecting the brand identity in every aspect of the business, entrepreneurs can create a brand that captures the attention and loyalty of their target audience. A strong brand identity will not only differentiate a business from its competitors but also build trust and credibility among customers. With a solid brand identity in place, start-ups and business owners can navigate the challenging entrepreneurial journey with confidence and achieve their goals.

Creating a Marketing Plan

In today's competitive business landscape, having a well-defined marketing plan is crucial for the success of any startup or business. A marketing plan serves as a roadmap, guiding entrepreneurs and business owners towards achieving their goals by effectively promoting their products or services to their target audience. This subchapter will delve into the key components of creating a comprehensive marketing plan, providing valuable insights and strategies for start-ups, business owners, and entrepreneurs in the niche of business coaching and mentoring.

1. Defining Your Target Market:
Before embarking on any marketing activities, it is essential to thoroughly understand your target market. Identify the demographics, psychographics, and behaviors of your ideal customers. By defining your target market, you can tailor your marketing efforts to reach the right audience with the right message, thereby maximizing your return on investment.

2. Setting Marketing Objectives:

Clearly outline the marketing objectives you aim to achieve. Whether it is increasing brand awareness, generating leads, or driving sales, setting SMART (Specific, Measurable, Achievable, Relevant, and Time-bound) goals will help you stay focused and measure your progress.

3. Conducting Market Research:

Conducting thorough market research is crucial for understanding market trends, competitor analysis, and customer preferences. This research will enable you to identify gaps in the market and develop unique selling propositions that differentiate your products or services from the competition.

4. Developing a Marketing Strategy:

Based on your research findings, develop a comprehensive marketing strategy that outlines the tactics you will employ to reach and engage your target audience. This may include digital marketing, social media campaigns, content marketing, public relations, or traditional advertising. Align your marketing strategy with your brand's values, ensuring consistency across all channels.

5. Implementing and Evaluating:

Once your marketing strategy is in place, it's time to execute your plan. Monitor and evaluate the performance of your marketing initiatives, utilizing key performance indicators (KPIs) to measure success. Make adjustments as necessary to optimize your marketing efforts and achieve your desired outcomes.

By creating a well-crafted marketing plan, start-ups, business owners, and entrepreneurs in the business coaching and mentoring niche can effectively position their brand, connect with their target audience, and achieve their business goals. Remember, a marketing plan is not a one-time activity but an ongoing process that requires constant evaluation and adaptation to stay ahead in the ever-evolving marketplace.

Utilizing Digital Marketing Channels

In today's digital age, the success of any business heavily relies on its ability to effectively utilize digital marketing channels. With the vast array of online platforms available, businesses have the opportunity to reach a wider audience, engage with potential customers, and ultimately drive growth. This subchapter will provide an in-depth understanding of various digital marketing channels and how start-ups, business owners, and entrepreneurs can harness their potential to achieve their goals.

First and foremost, social media platforms have become a crucial component of any digital marketing strategy. With billions of active users, platforms like Facebook, Instagram, Twitter, and LinkedIn offer immense potential for businesses to create brand awareness, engage with customers, and drive conversions. Whether it's through organic posts, paid advertisements, or influencer collaborations, businesses can leverage social media to build a loyal customer base and boost their online presence.

Another essential digital marketing channel is search engine optimization (SEO). By optimizing their websites and content for search engines, businesses can improve their visibility in search engine results pages and attract organic traffic. This subchapter will delve into the fundamentals of SEO, including keyword research, on-page optimization, and link building strategies, providing start-ups and business owners with the tools to enhance their website's search engine rankings and increase their chances of being discovered by potential customers.

Email marketing is yet another powerful digital marketing channel that allows businesses to reach their target audience directly. By building an email list and crafting personalized, engaging content, businesses can nurture leads, build customer relationships, and drive conversions. This subchapter will explore effective email marketing strategies, including segmentation, automation, and A/B testing, enabling entrepreneurs to create impactful email campaigns that yield tangible results.

Additionally, pay-per-click (PPC) advertising is an indispensable digital marketing channel that can generate immediate results. From search engine advertising to display ads and remarketing campaigns, businesses can strategically place their ads in front of their target audience, driving traffic and increasing conversions. This subchapter will guide start-ups and business owners on how to set up and optimize PPC campaigns, ensuring they maximize their return on investment.

In conclusion, digital marketing channels are essential tools for start-ups, business owners, and entrepreneurs to achieve their goals. By effectively utilizing social media, SEO, email marketing, and PPC advertising, businesses can expand their reach, engage with their target audience, and drive growth. Understanding the intricacies of each channel and implementing the right strategies will empower entrepreneurs to navigate the digital landscape successfully and stay ahead of the competition.

Chapter 9: Sales and Customer Acquisition

Identifying and Targeting Potential Customers

One of the fundamental aspects of running a successful business is identifying and targeting potential customers. Without a clear understanding of who your target audience is, your marketing efforts may fall flat, and your business may struggle to gain traction. In this subchapter, we will explore the importance of identifying your potential customers and provide practical strategies to effectively reach them.

To begin, let's emphasize the significance of knowing your target audience. Understanding who your potential customers are allows you to tailor your products or services specifically to their needs and preferences. This knowledge enables you to develop effective marketing campaigns, create compelling messaging, and differentiate yourself from competitors. By identifying your potential customers, you can prioritize your resources and allocate them in the most efficient and cost-effective manner.

To identify your potential customers, start by conducting thorough market research. Explore demographic data, such as age, gender, income level, and geographic location, to gain insights into your target audience's characteristics. Additionally, consider psychographic factors, including interests, values, and lifestyles, to better understand their motivations and preferences. This research can be done through surveys, focus groups, or analyzing existing data sources.

Once you have identified your potential customers, it's essential to target them effectively. Develop a comprehensive marketing strategy that aligns with your target audience's preferred communication channels. This may include utilizing social media platforms, email marketing, content marketing, or traditional advertising methods, depending on your niche and target market.

Tailor your messaging to resonate with your potential customers, highlighting the unique value your products or services offer.

Furthermore, consider implementing customer segmentation techniques. Group your potential customers based on common characteristics or behaviors, allowing you to create personalized marketing campaigns that address their specific needs. This approach helps you reach a wider audience while still delivering tailored messages.

Lastly, continuously monitor and evaluate the effectiveness of your marketing efforts. Utilize analytics tools to measure engagement, conversion rates, and customer feedback. Regularly review and refine your strategies based on these insights, ensuring that you are continuously improving your targeting efforts.

In conclusion, identifying and targeting potential customers is a critical component of any successful business. By understanding who your target audience is and developing effective strategies to reach them, you can maximize your marketing efforts and drive business growth. Remember to conduct thorough market research, tailor your messaging, and continuously evaluate and refine your strategies to stay ahead in today's competitive business landscape.

Building a Sales Funnel

In the world of business, the ability to generate and convert leads into loyal customers is crucial for success. This is where a sales funnel comes into play. A sales funnel is a strategic process that guides potential customers through various stages until they make a purchase. In this subchapter, we will explore the importance of building a sales funnel and provide practical tips for start-ups, business owners, and entrepreneurs in the niches of business coaching and mentoring.

A well-designed sales funnel allows businesses to streamline their marketing efforts, attract the right audience, and maximize conversions. It begins with the awareness stage, where potential customers first discover your brand. This can be achieved through various marketing channels such as social media, content marketing, and advertising. The goal is to create a strong first impression and grab their attention.

Once potential customers are aware of your brand, the next stage is interest. Here, you need to nurture their curiosity by providing valuable content, engaging with them through personalized communication, and demonstrating expertise in your field. This helps to build trust and establish your brand as a reliable solution to their needs.

The third stage is decision-making, where potential customers evaluate their options and make a purchasing decision. This is where you need to showcase the unique selling points of your product or service, offer compelling incentives, and address any concerns or objections they may have. Providing social proof, such as testimonials or case studies, can also help to convince them of your credibility.

Finally, the last stage is action, where potential customers become paying customers. This can be facilitated through clear and easy-to-use calls-to-action, streamlined checkout processes, and a seamless user experience. After the purchase, it's crucial to continue nurturing the customer relationship to encourage repeat purchases and foster brand loyalty.

To build an effective sales funnel, start-ups, business owners, and entrepreneurs should focus on understanding their target audience, developing compelling and relevant messaging, and leveraging technology to automate and optimize the funnel. Regularly analyzing and measuring the performance of each stage is also essential for identifying areas for improvement and making data-driven decisions.

In conclusion, building a sales funnel is an integral part of any business's growth strategy. By implementing a well-defined process that guides potential customers through each stage of the buying journey, start-ups, business owners, and entrepreneurs in the field of business coaching and mentoring can increase their chances of success and achieve their goals.

Sales Techniques and Closing Deals

In the world of business, one of the most crucial skills every entrepreneur, start-up, and business owner must possess is the ability to close deals effectively. The success of any venture heavily relies on the ability to sell products or services to customers, making the mastery of sales techniques vital for sustainable growth and profitability. This subchapter aims to equip start-ups, business owners, and entrepreneurs with valuable insights and strategies to enhance their sales techniques and improve their ability to close deals successfully.

1. Understanding the Sales Process:
Before delving into specific techniques, it is essential to grasp the fundamentals of the sales process. From prospecting to closing, understanding each stage and its importance allows entrepreneurs to navigate the journey effectively. By identifying potential customers, nurturing relationships, and addressing their needs, entrepreneurs can create a personalized sales approach that resonates with clients.

2. Building Rapport and Trust:
Establishing a strong rapport and building trust with potential customers is vital for successful sales. Entrepreneurs should focus on active listening, empathizing with the client's challenges, and providing tailored solutions. By demonstrating expertise, credibility, and a genuine interest in solving their problems, entrepreneurs can build trust and foster long-term relationships.

3. Effective Communication and Presentation Skills:
Effective communication and presentation skills are instrumental in capturing the attention of potential customers. Entrepreneurs should learn to articulate their value proposition clearly, highlighting the unique benefits their products or services offer. Presentations should be engaging, concise, and tailored to the needs and preferences of the target audience.

4. Overcoming Objections:
In the sales process, objections from potential customers are common. Entrepreneurs must develop strategies to address objections effectively and turn them into opportunities. By actively listening, empathizing, and providing compelling answers, entrepreneurs can alleviate concerns and build confidence in their offerings.

5. Closing Techniques:
Closing a deal is the ultimate goal of any sales process. Entrepreneurs should learn various closing techniques to increase their chances of success. Whether it's the assumptive close, the alternative close, or the trial close, understanding how and when to employ these techniques can make a significant difference in sealing the deal.

6. Negotiation Skills:
Negotiation is a crucial aspect of closing deals. Entrepreneurs must master negotiation skills to ensure mutually beneficial outcomes. By understanding the needs and priorities of both parties, entrepreneurs can reach agreements that satisfy both their customers and their own business objectives.

By mastering these sales techniques and effectively closing deals, start-ups, business owners, and entrepreneurs can accelerate their business growth and achieve their goals. Continuous learning, practice, and refinement of these skills will provide a competitive edge in the dynamic and ever-evolving business landscape.

Chapter 10: Scaling and Growing Your Business

Strategies for Scaling Up

Scaling up a business is an exciting yet challenging phase for start-ups, business owners, and entrepreneurs. It is a crucial step towards achieving growth and reaching new heights. However, it requires careful planning, strategic decision-making, and efficient execution. This subchapter will explore some effective strategies for scaling up, providing valuable insights and guidance to entrepreneurs in their journey towards business expansion.

1. Set Clear Goals: Before embarking on the scaling-up journey, it is crucial to define clear goals and objectives. These goals will serve as a compass, guiding entrepreneurs in making informed decisions and prioritizing their resources effectively.

2. Streamline Operations: To scale up successfully, entrepreneurs must review their existing processes and identify any bottlenecks or inefficiencies. Streamlining operations, automating tasks, and implementing technology solutions can significantly enhance productivity and pave the way for growth.

3. Build a Strong Team: Scaling up requires a strong and capable team. Entrepreneurs should focus on attracting top talent, hiring individuals who align with the company's culture and values. Delegating responsibilities and empowering employees will foster a collaborative and high-performance work environment.

4. Expand Market Reach: Scaling up often involves expanding into new markets or reaching a broader customer base. Entrepreneurs should conduct market research, identify target segments, and develop effective marketing strategies to penetrate new territories successfully.

5. Establish Strategic Partnerships: Collaborating with strategic partners can provide access to new resources, expertise, and customer networks. Entrepreneurs should actively seek partnerships with complementary businesses or industry leaders to accelerate growth and increase market presence.

6. Leverage Technology: Technology plays a pivotal role in scaling up businesses. Entrepreneurs should adopt innovative tools and solutions that streamline operations, enhance customer experiences, and enable data-driven decision-making.

7. Secure Adequate Funding: Scaling up often requires additional capital. Entrepreneurs should explore various funding options, such as venture capital, angel investors, or business loans, to secure the necessary financial resources for expansion.

8. Embrace Continuous Learning: The journey of scaling up is a continuous learning process. Entrepreneurs should stay updated with industry trends, attend conferences, join networking events, and seek mentorship or business coaching to gain valuable insights and stay ahead of the competition.

Scaling up a business is an exciting and challenging endeavor. By implementing these strategies, start-ups, business owners, and entrepreneurs can navigate the complexities of growth, maximize their potential, and achieve their goals in a sustainable and successful manner.

Expanding into New Markets

As an entrepreneur or business owner, one of the key drivers for growth and success is expanding into new markets. This subchapter will guide you through the process of identifying, evaluating, and entering new markets to help you achieve your goals.

When it comes to expanding into new markets, it is crucial to conduct thorough market research. This involves identifying potential target markets, understanding their needs and preferences, and evaluating the competition in those markets. By gathering this information, you can make informed decisions about which markets offer the best opportunities for your business.

Once you have identified potential new markets, it is essential to develop a comprehensive market entry strategy. This strategy should outline the steps you will take to enter the market successfully, including pricing strategies, distribution channels, and marketing tactics. It should also consider any legal or regulatory requirements specific to the new market.

In some cases, entering a new market may require adapting your product or service to meet the needs of the local customers. This may involve making modifications to the existing product or developing new offerings altogether. By tailoring your offerings to the preferences of the new market, you increase your chances of success and customer satisfaction.

Expanding into new markets also requires careful financial planning. You need to assess the costs associated with entering the new market, including market research, product development, marketing, and distribution expenses. Additionally, you should consider the potential return on investment and develop a realistic revenue forecast for the new market.

To ensure a smooth entry into new markets, it is often beneficial to seek guidance from business coaches and mentors. These professionals can provide valuable insights and advice based on their experience in similar situations. They can help you identify potential challenges, develop strategies to overcome them, and provide ongoing support as you navigate the complexities of entering new markets.

Expanding into new markets is an exciting opportunity for growth and can lead to increased profitability and brand recognition. However, it requires careful planning, research, and execution. By following the steps outlined in this subchapter and leveraging the expertise of business coaches and mentors, you can confidently expand into new markets and achieve your entrepreneurial goals.

Managing Growth Challenges

One of the most exciting yet daunting times for start-ups, business owners, and entrepreneurs is when their ventures experience rapid growth. While growth is often seen as a sign of success, it can also bring about numerous challenges that can hinder progress if not managed effectively. In this subchapter, we will explore some of the common growth challenges faced by businesses and provide practical strategies to overcome them.

1. Scaling Operations: As your business expands, it is crucial to scale your operations accordingly. This involves evaluating and upgrading your infrastructure, processes, and systems to accommodate increased demand. Implementing efficient workflows, leveraging technology, and outsourcing non-core tasks can help streamline operations and maintain customer satisfaction during periods of growth.

2. Hiring and Retaining Talent: As your team grows, finding and retaining top talent becomes essential. Clearly defining your company's values, culture, and growth opportunities can attract the right individuals. Developing a robust recruitment strategy, conducting thorough interviews, and offering competitive compensation packages are key to securing and retaining skilled employees.

3. Financial Management: Rapid growth often requires significant financial resources. Managing cash flow, securing funding, and forecasting revenue becomes crucial during this phase. Working closely with financial advisors, creating a detailed budget, and exploring different financing options will help ensure your business has the necessary capital to sustain and thrive during growth.

4. Maintaining Customer Satisfaction: Expanding your customer base is an exciting prospect, but it also presents the challenge of meeting increased demands while maintaining customer satisfaction. Focusing on delivering exceptional customer service, continuously improving products or services, and implementing effective communication channels can help create loyal customers who will support your growth trajectory.

5. Leadership and Delegation: As your business grows, it is vital to adapt your leadership style and delegate responsibilities to capable individuals. Effective delegation allows you to focus on strategic decision-making and empowers your team members to take ownership and contribute to the company's growth. Developing leadership skills, fostering a culture of trust and accountability, and providing ongoing training are essential for managing growth challenges.

6. Market Expansion: Scaling your business often involves expanding into new markets or launching new products/services. Conducting thorough market research, understanding customer needs, and developing a robust marketing strategy will help facilitate successful expansion. It is crucial to adapt your offerings to suit each target market's unique requirements while maintaining consistency in your brand messaging.

Managing growth challenges is critical for start-ups, business owners, and entrepreneurs seeking sustainable success. By proactively addressing these challenges, implementing effective strategies, and seeking guidance from experienced business coaches or mentors, you can navigate the complexities of growth and emerge as a stronger, more resilient business. Remember that growth is a journey, and with the right mindset and strategies, you can overcome any obstacle that comes your way.

Chapter 11: Navigating Challenges and Overcoming Obstacles

Dealing with Failure and Setbacks

Failure and setbacks are an inevitable part of the entrepreneurial journey. The road to success is filled with ups and downs, and how you handle these challenges can make all the difference. In this subchapter, we will explore strategies and techniques for effectively dealing with failure and setbacks, helping start-ups, business owners, and entrepreneurs navigate through these tough times.

1. Embrace a Growth Mindset: Adopting a growth mindset is crucial when facing failure. Instead of viewing setbacks as permanent or personal, see them as opportunities for learning and growth. Understand that failure is a stepping stone to success and an essential part of the entrepreneurial process.

2. Reflect and Learn: After a setback, take the time to reflect on what went wrong and identify the lessons learned. Analyze the situation objectively, without blaming yourself or others. By understanding the root causes of failure, you can make necessary adjustments and improve your chances of success in the future.

3. Seek Support: Surround yourself with a network of mentors, coaches, and fellow entrepreneurs who can provide guidance and support during challenging times. They can offer valuable insights, share their own experiences, and help you regain perspective when things go awry.

4. Adapt and Pivot: In the face of failure, be willing to adapt and pivot your business strategy. Sometimes, setbacks serve as catalysts for innovation and uncover new opportunities. Stay open-minded, be flexible, and embrace change to overcome obstacles and move forward.

5. Take Care of Yourself: Failure and setbacks can be emotionally draining, so it's important to prioritize self-care. Maintain a healthy work-life balance, engage in activities that bring you joy, and practice mindfulness or meditation to stay centered and resilient during difficult times.

6. Set Realistic Expectations: Unrealistic expectations can set you up for failure. It's essential to set realistic goals and timelines for your business, allowing for setbacks and unforeseen challenges. This way, you'll be better prepared mentally and emotionally to handle setbacks when they occur.

7. Stay Positive and Persistent: Maintaining a positive mindset is crucial when dealing with failure and setbacks. Surround yourself with positive influences, celebrate small wins, and remind yourself of your ultimate vision. Persistence is key; keep pushing forward, even when faced with obstacles.

Remember, failure is not the end, but rather an opportunity to learn, grow, and improve. By adopting the right mindset, seeking support, and staying resilient, you can overcome setbacks and continue your journey towards entrepreneurial success.

[Word Count: 298 words]

Handling Competition and Market Shifts

In today's rapidly evolving business landscape, competition is inevitable. As a start-up, business owner, or entrepreneur, it is crucial to understand how to effectively handle competition and adapt to market shifts. This subchapter explores strategies and insights that will guide you in navigating these challenges and staying ahead of the curve.

Competition is healthy and can drive innovation and growth. It pushes businesses to continuously improve their products, services, and overall customer experience. However, it can also pose significant threats if not handled strategically. The first step in handling competition is to thoroughly understand your market and identify your unique value proposition. By clearly defining your target audience, understanding their needs, and clearly differentiating yourself from competitors, you can create a strong competitive advantage.

Market shifts are another aspect that start-ups, business owners, and entrepreneurs must be prepared to handle. Changes in technology, consumer behavior, and economic conditions can significantly impact your business. It is vital to stay well-informed and proactive in assessing these shifts to make timely adjustments. Regularly monitoring industry trends, conducting market research, and engaging with customers will help you identify potential shifts early on. By doing so, you can adapt your strategies, product offerings, and business models to meet the changing demands of the market.

To effectively handle competition and market shifts, business coaching and mentoring can be invaluable. Working with experienced mentors or coaches who have successfully navigated similar challenges can provide you with invaluable guidance and insights. They can help you develop effective strategies, make informed decisions, and offer support during times of uncertainty.

Furthermore, fostering a culture of continuous learning and innovation within your organization is key. Encouraging employees to stay updated with industry trends, fostering a mindset of adaptability, and providing opportunities for training and development will enable your team to be agile and responsive to competition and market shifts.

In conclusion, handling competition and market shifts is a crucial aspect of running a successful business. By understanding your market, differentiating yourself, staying informed about industry trends, and seeking guidance from business coaches and mentors, you can navigate these challenges and seize opportunities for growth. Embrace competition as a catalyst for innovation, and adapt to market shifts to stay ahead of the curve. Remember, success lies in your ability to anticipate change, adapt quickly, and continuously strive for improvement.

Overcoming Fear and Taking Calculated Risks

Fear is a natural and common emotion that often holds us back from reaching our full potential as entrepreneurs. It can prevent us from taking risks and seizing opportunities that could lead to great success. However, in order to grow and thrive in the competitive world of business, it is essential to learn how to overcome fear and take calculated risks.

In this subchapter, we will explore the importance of overcoming fear, understanding the different types of fear that entrepreneurs face, and strategies for taking calculated risks that can lead to business growth and achievement of goals.

Fear can manifest in various forms for entrepreneurs. It could be fear of failure, fear of rejection, fear of financial loss, or fear of the unknown. These fears can paralyze us and hinder our ability to take action. However, it is important to recognize that fear is a normal part of the entrepreneurial journey. By acknowledging our fears and understanding their underlying causes, we can begin to address and overcome them.

One effective strategy for overcoming fear is to develop a growth mindset. This involves reframing failures and setbacks as learning opportunities rather than personal shortcomings. By embracing a mindset that views challenges as stepping stones to success, entrepreneurs can build resilience and become more willing to take risks.

Another valuable approach is to seek support from business coaches and mentors. These individuals have experienced similar fears and challenges and can provide guidance and encouragement. They can help entrepreneurs assess risks, develop contingency plans, and provide a fresh perspective when fear threatens to cloud judgment.

Taking calculated risks is an essential aspect of entrepreneurship. By carefully evaluating potential risks and rewards, entrepreneurs can make informed decisions that have the potential to yield significant benefits. This involves conducting thorough market research, analyzing competition, and assessing financial implications. It also requires setting clear goals and establishing a roadmap to mitigate risks and maximize opportunities.

In conclusion, fear can be a significant barrier to success for entrepreneurs. However, by understanding the different types of fear, developing a growth mindset, seeking support from mentors, and taking calculated risks, entrepreneurs can overcome fear and unlock their full potential. Embracing fear as a catalyst for growth and viewing risks as opportunities can lead to significant achievements on the entrepreneurial journey.

Chapter 12: Maintaining Work-Life Balance and Wellness

Strategies for Work-Life Balance

In today's fast-paced business world, achieving a healthy work-life balance has become increasingly challenging for start-ups, business owners, and entrepreneurs. The constant demands of running a business, combined with personal responsibilities, can often leave individuals feeling overwhelmed and burnt out. However, by implementing effective strategies, entrepreneurs can find harmony between their professional and personal lives, leading to increased productivity, satisfaction, and overall success.

1. Prioritize and delegate: As an entrepreneur, it's crucial to identify your most important tasks and focus on them. Delegate non-essential tasks to capable team members or consider outsourcing to free up your time and minimize stress.

2. Set boundaries: Establish clear boundaries between work and personal life. Create designated work hours and stick to them, avoiding the temptation to constantly check emails or respond to work-related matters during personal time.

3. Schedule downtime: Just as you schedule business meetings and appointments, make it a priority to schedule downtime for yourself. Whether it's spending time with family, pursuing hobbies, or simply relaxing, having scheduled breaks will help you recharge and avoid burnout.

4. Embrace technology: Leverage technology to streamline tasks and increase efficiency. Utilize project management tools, communication apps, and automation software to save time and reduce manual labor, enabling you to focus on more important aspects of your business and personal life.

5. Seek support: Surround yourself with a strong support system, both personally and professionally. Engage in networking events, join entrepreneur communities, and seek out mentors or business coaches who can provide guidance and support. Having someone to lean on during challenging times can make a significant difference in maintaining work-life balance.

6. Practice self-care: Take care of your physical and mental well-being. Incorporate regular exercise, healthy eating, and adequate sleep into your routine. Prioritize self-care activities such as meditation, yoga, or hobbies that help you relax and rejuvenate.

7. Manage expectations: As an entrepreneur, it's important to set realistic expectations for both yourself and those around you. Communicate openly with your team, clients, and loved ones about your availability, deadlines, and boundaries to avoid unnecessary stress and frustration.

Remember, achieving work-life balance is an ongoing process that requires conscious effort and adaptation. By implementing these strategies, you can create a harmonious integration of work and personal life, leading to increased happiness, fulfillment, and success in both realms.

Prioritizing Self-Care and Mental Health

In the fast-paced world of entrepreneurship, it's easy to get caught up in the hustle and bustle of building a successful business. However, amidst the chaos, it's crucial not to neglect one of the most important aspects of your journey: self-care and mental health. In this subchapter, we will explore the significance of prioritizing self-care and mental well-being for start-ups, business owners, and entrepreneurs.

Running a business can be a rollercoaster ride, filled with highs and lows. It is during these challenging times that your mental health can take a toll. As an entrepreneur, it's essential to recognize that your mental well-being directly impacts your business's success. Neglecting self-care can lead to burnout, decreased productivity, and even the collapse of your venture.

First and foremost, it's crucial to establish a self-care routine that works for you. This can include activities such as exercise, meditation, journaling, or spending quality time with loved ones. Taking care of your physical health through regular exercise and a balanced diet not only boosts your energy levels but also enhances your mental well-being.

Additionally, carving out time for relaxation and leisure activities allows you to recharge and maintain a healthy work-life balance. Remember, self-care is not a luxury but a necessity for long-term success. By prioritizing self-care, you'll have more energy, focus, and resilience to tackle the challenges that come your way.

Furthermore, seeking support from mentors or business coaches who understand the entrepreneurial journey is invaluable. Surrounding yourself with a network of like-minded individuals who can provide guidance and support can significantly impact your mental health. Sharing your challenges and successes with others who have experienced similar situations can provide a sense of belonging and alleviate feelings of isolation.

Moreover, don't hesitate to seek professional help if needed. Mental health should never be stigmatized, and seeking therapy or counseling can be immensely beneficial. A trained professional can help you navigate the stress, anxiety, and pressures that come with running a business.

Remember, your mental health is an asset, not a liability. By prioritizing self-care, you are investing in your business's success. Take the time to nurture your well-being, develop healthy habits, and seek support when needed. By doing so, you're not only benefiting yourself but also setting a positive example for your team and creating a culture of self-care within your organization.

Building a Support Network

One of the most important factors in achieving success as an entrepreneur is building a strong support network. As the saying goes, "No man is an island," and this is especially true in the world of business. Surrounding yourself with the right people who can provide guidance, support, and mentorship can make all the difference in your entrepreneurial journey.

Start-ups, business owners, and entrepreneurs often face unique challenges and obstacles that can be overwhelming to navigate alone. That's where building a support network comes in. By connecting with like-minded individuals who understand your struggles and can offer valuable advice, you can gain the confidence and knowledge needed to overcome any hurdles.

One of the best ways to build a support network is through business coaching and mentoring. These professionals have the expertise and experience to guide you through the ups and downs of entrepreneurship. A business coach can help you define your goals, develop a solid business plan, and hold you accountable for your progress. They can also provide valuable insights and strategies to help you overcome specific challenges you may be facing.

Mentors, on the other hand, are individuals who have already achieved success in their respective fields. They can offer you invaluable advice based on their own experiences, helping you avoid common pitfalls and make sound business decisions. Finding the right mentor can be a game-changer for your entrepreneurial journey, as they can provide you with guidance and support that goes beyond what a business coach can offer.

In addition to coaching and mentoring, networking events and industry conferences are excellent opportunities to build a support network. These events bring together like-minded individuals who are all striving for success in their respective fields. By attending such events, you can meet potential mentors, partners, and even clients who can contribute to your growth and success.

Remember, building a support network is not just about receiving help; it's also about giving back to others. As you progress on your entrepreneurial journey, don't hesitate to offer support and advice to those who are just starting out. By sharing your own experiences and lessons learned, you can help aspiring entrepreneurs overcome their own challenges and create a thriving community of support.

In conclusion, building a support network is crucial for start-ups, business owners, and entrepreneurs. Through business coaching, mentoring, networking events, and giving back, you can surround yourself with the right people who can provide the guidance, support, and mentorship needed to achieve your goals. Don't underestimate the power of a strong support network – it can be the catalyst for your success as an entrepreneur.

Chapter 13: Leveraging Technology and Innovation

Embracing Digital Transformation

In today's rapidly evolving business landscape, embracing digital transformation has become a non-negotiable requirement for startups, business owners, and entrepreneurs alike. The ever-increasing reliance on technology and the internet has completely reshaped the way we conduct business, communicate with customers, and stay ahead of competitors. This subchapter explores the importance of embracing digital transformation and provides valuable insights for entrepreneurs seeking to leverage its potential.

Digital transformation refers to the integration of digital technologies into all aspects of a business, fundamentally changing how it operates and delivers value to customers. As we move further into the digital age, businesses that fail to adapt risk falling behind and becoming obsolete in an increasingly competitive market.

One of the key advantages of embracing digital transformation is the ability to reach a wider audience and target customers more effectively. Through platforms like social media, search engines, and online advertising, startups and business owners can connect with their target audience directly, creating personalized experiences and building lasting relationships. Furthermore, leveraging digital tools and analytics allows entrepreneurs to gain valuable insights into customer behavior, preferences, and market trends, enabling them to make data-driven decisions and optimize their strategies.

Digital transformation also offers significant cost savings and operational efficiencies. By automating repetitive tasks, streamlining workflows, and adopting cloud computing solutions, businesses can reduce overhead costs and improve productivity. Additionally, digital tools enable remote collaboration, allowing startups to tap into a global talent pool and overcome geographical limitations.

However, embracing digital transformation requires more than just adopting technology. It requires a mindset shift and a willingness to adapt to changing market dynamics. Entrepreneurs must be open to learning and upgrading their skills, as well as fostering a culture of innovation and agility within their organizations.

To successfully embrace digital transformation, startups and business owners can benefit from seeking guidance from experienced business coaches and mentors. These professionals can provide valuable insights, share best practices, and help navigate the complexities of the digital landscape. They can also assist in identifying and implementing the most relevant digital strategies for each specific business, ensuring a smooth transition and maximizing the potential for growth and success.

In conclusion, embracing digital transformation is no longer a choice but a necessity for startups, business owners, and entrepreneurs. By leveraging the power of digital technologies, businesses can reach a wider audience, improve operational efficiency, and gain a competitive edge. With the guidance of experienced business coaches and mentors, entrepreneurs can navigate the digital landscape successfully and achieve their goals in this ever-evolving business world.

Harnessing the Power of Data Analytics

In today's fast-paced and highly competitive business world, data analytics has emerged as a crucial tool for start-ups, business owners, and entrepreneurs. The ability to collect, analyze, and interpret data provides valuable insights that can drive business growth, improve decision-making processes, and unlock new opportunities. This subchapter will explore how harnessing the power of data analytics can revolutionize your business and help you achieve your goals.

Data analytics refers to the process of examining raw data to uncover patterns, correlations, and trends. By leveraging advanced technology and analytical tools, businesses can gain a deep understanding of customer behavior, market trends, and operational efficiency. This knowledge is invaluable for making strategic decisions, identifying untapped markets, and optimizing business operations.

For start-ups and entrepreneurs, data analytics can be a game-changer. By analyzing customer data and feedback, start-ups can tailor their products or services to meet customer needs more effectively. This customer-centric approach enhances customer satisfaction, builds brand loyalty, and ultimately leads to increased sales and revenue.

Additionally, data analytics enables businesses to identify and target specific customer segments more accurately. By understanding customer preferences and behavior, entrepreneurs can create personalized marketing campaigns that resonate with their target audience. This personalized approach not only maximizes marketing ROI but also strengthens customer engagement and brand perception.

Business owners can also leverage data analytics to optimize their operations. By analyzing data related to inventory management, production processes, and supply chain operations, entrepreneurs can identify inefficiencies and streamline their operations. This leads to cost savings, improved productivity, and enhanced customer satisfaction.

Furthermore, data analytics plays a vital role in risk management and fraud detection. By analyzing patterns and anomalies in financial transactions, businesses can identify potential risks and take appropriate preventive measures. This proactive approach not only safeguards the business but also enhances its reputation and builds trust with customers and stakeholders.

However, harnessing the power of data analytics requires more than just collecting and analyzing data. It requires a comprehensive understanding of data privacy and security, as well as the ability to interpret and act upon the insights gained from the data. Therefore, businesses should consider investing in the necessary technology, talent, and training to effectively utilize data analytics.

In conclusion, data analytics has become an indispensable tool for start-ups, business owners, and entrepreneurs. By harnessing the power of data analytics, businesses can gain valuable insights, make informed decisions, optimize operations, and drive business growth. Embracing data analytics is no longer an option; it is a necessity for those who want to stay ahead in today's dynamic business landscape.

Adopting New Technologies for Efficiency

In today's fast-paced and ever-evolving business landscape, staying ahead of the curve is crucial for the success of any start-up, business owner, or entrepreneur. One of the most effective ways to gain a competitive edge and increase efficiency is by adopting new technologies. Embracing these advancements can revolutionize your operations, streamline processes, and ultimately propel your business towards achieving its goals.

In this subchapter, we will explore the importance of adopting new technologies for efficiency and how it can positively impact your business. We will delve into the benefits, challenges, and strategies for successful implementation.

The benefits of adopting new technologies are manifold. Firstly, it allows you to automate repetitive tasks, freeing up valuable time and resources that can be redirected towards more strategic and revenue-generating activities. Additionally, technology-driven solutions can enhance communication and collaboration within your team, leading to improved productivity and innovation. Moreover, the right technology can provide invaluable data insights, enabling you to make data-driven decisions and gain a deeper understanding of your target audience.

However, implementing new technologies is not without its challenges. It requires careful planning, effective change management, and adequate training for your team. Resistance to change is common, and it is crucial to address any concerns and provide support to ensure a smooth transition. Moreover, selecting the right technologies for your specific business needs is vital. This subchapter will guide you through the process of evaluating and selecting the most suitable technologies for your business, taking into account factors such as scalability, compatibility, and cost-effectiveness.

To successfully adopt new technologies, it is essential to develop a comprehensive strategy. We will provide you with a step-by-step roadmap for implementation, covering aspects such as planning, budgeting, and risk management. Additionally, we will discuss the importance of continuous learning and staying updated on emerging technologies to maintain your competitive edge.

As a business coaching and mentoring resource, we understand the challenges entrepreneurs face when embracing technological advancements. Through this subchapter, we aim to equip you with the knowledge and tools necessary to navigate the ever-changing technological landscape confidently.

By adopting new technologies for efficiency, you can transform your business, maximize productivity, and stay ahead of the competition. Whether you are a start-up or an established business owner, this subchapter will serve as your guide to harnessing the power of technology and achieving your business goals. Embrace the future and let technology be your catalyst for success.

Chapter 14: Success Stories and Lessons Learned

Inspiring Success Stories from Entrepreneurs

Introduction:

In the world of entrepreneurship, success stories serve as a beacon of hope and motivation for aspiring start-ups and business owners. These tales of triumph against all odds not only inspire but also provide valuable lessons and insights. In this subchapter, we will delve into a collection of inspiring success stories from entrepreneurs who have navigated the challenging path of business ownership. These stories will ignite your entrepreneurial spirit and encourage you to pursue your goals with unwavering determination.

1. The Story of Sarah: Overcoming Adversity to Create a Multi-Million Dollar Business

Sarah's journey began with limited resources and a turbulent personal life. However, her unwavering determination and relentless work ethic propelled her forward. Through her innovative ideas and strategic decision-making, she transformed her small start-up into a multi-million dollar empire. Sarah's story teaches us the importance of resilience, adaptability, and seizing opportunities when they arise.

2. John's Path to Global Recognition: From a Garage to an International Brand

John's story is a classic tale of starting from scratch. With nothing but a brilliant idea and a passion for his craft, he began his business in his own garage. Through sheer dedication and a commitment to excellence, John's brand gained international recognition. His story serves as a reminder that no dream is too big and that hard work and perseverance can lead to incredible achievements.

3. Mary's Socially Conscious Start-Up: Empowering Communities Through Business

Mary's entrepreneurial journey was driven by her desire to make a positive impact on society. With a vision of empowering underprivileged communities, she founded a socially conscious start-up. By integrating her passion for social causes with her business acumen, Mary not only created a successful venture but also made a significant difference in the lives of many. Her story inspires us to align our business goals with our personal values.

Conclusion:

These inspiring success stories highlight the resilience, determination, and innovation required to achieve entrepreneurial success. They remind us that setbacks are merely stepping stones to success and that every obstacle presents an opportunity for growth. Whether you are just starting your entrepreneurial journey or seeking guidance as an existing business owner, these stories will motivate you to embrace challenges, think outside the box, and pursue your dreams relentlessly. Remember, every successful entrepreneur started somewhere, and their stories can serve as your roadmap to achievement.

Key Lessons Learned from Successful Business Owners

In the journey of entrepreneurship, learning from those who have already achieved success can be invaluable. Successful business owners have faced numerous challenges, overcome obstacles, and achieved their goals. Their experiences and insights can serve as a guiding light for start-ups, business owners, and entrepreneurs looking to achieve similar success.

1. Embrace Failure as a Learning Opportunity: One common lesson learned by successful business owners is the importance of embracing failure. They understand that failure is not the end but a stepping stone towards success. Each failure provides an opportunity to learn, grow, and refine strategies for future success.

2. Build a Strong Support Network: Successful business owners recognize the significance of surrounding themselves with a strong support network. This

network can include mentors, coaches, industry peers, and trusted advisors. Having a support system that provides guidance, feedback, and accountability can accelerate growth and help navigate challenges.

3. Continuous Learning and Adaptability: Entrepreneurs who have achieved success understand that learning is a lifelong process. They prioritize continuous learning and stay updated with industry trends, technological advancements, and best practices. Being adaptable and open to change allows them to stay ahead of the competition and seize new opportunities.

4. Focus on Customer Needs: Successful business owners prioritize understanding their customers' needs and delivering value. They invest time and resources in market research, customer feedback, and building strong relationships. By putting customers first, they create loyal customer bases and build sustainable growth.

5. Develop a Strong Work Ethic: Hard work and dedication are common traits among successful business owners. They are willing to put in the time and effort needed to achieve their goals. They understand that success doesn't come overnight and are committed to consistently working towards their vision.

6. Effective Time Management: Time management is crucial for entrepreneurs, and successful business owners have mastered this skill. They prioritize tasks, delegate when necessary, and eliminate time-wasting activities. By effectively managing their time, they can focus on high-value activities that drive business growth.

7. Embrace Innovation and Take Calculated Risks: Successful business owners understand the importance of being innovative and taking calculated risks. They constantly seek opportunities for growth, explore new ideas, and are not afraid to step out of their comfort zones. By embracing innovation and taking calculated risks, they position themselves for success in a rapidly changing business landscape.

In conclusion, the lessons learned from successful business owners can provide invaluable insights for start-ups, business owners, and entrepreneurs. Embracing failure as a learning opportunity, building a strong support network, continuous learning, focusing on customer needs, developing a strong work ethic, effective time management, and embracing innovation are key lessons that can guide aspiring entrepreneurs towards achieving their goals. By applying these lessons, individuals in the business coaching and mentoring niche can help their clients navigate challenges, overcome obstacles, and achieve sustainable success.

Applying Lessons to Your Own Journey

As a start-up, business owner, or entrepreneur, embarking on your journey can be both exciting and overwhelming. You might find yourself constantly seeking guidance and support to help you navigate the challenges and uncertainties that lie ahead. This subchapter aims to provide you with valuable insights on applying lessons to your own journey, drawing from the experiences of successful entrepreneurs who have walked the path before you.

One of the most effective ways to accelerate your growth and success is by seeking out business coaching and mentoring. By connecting with experienced professionals who have already faced and conquered the obstacles you may encounter, you can gain valuable insights and advice to help propel your business forward. A good mentor can help you uncover blind spots, identify areas for improvement, and provide guidance on decision-making.

To make the most of your mentorship, it is essential to approach it with an open mind and a willingness to learn. Reflect on the lessons shared by successful entrepreneurs and adapt them to your own unique circumstances. Remember, while their experiences can serve as a guide, your own journey will have its own challenges and opportunities. Apply the lessons learned in a way that aligns with your vision and business goals.

Another crucial aspect of applying lessons to your journey is to embrace a growth mindset. Understand that failures and setbacks are inevitable, but they should be seen as learning opportunities rather than roadblocks. Embrace a mindset that encourages continuous improvement and resilience. Take risks, learn from your mistakes, and be open to pivoting when necessary.

Moreover, it is essential to stay informed about industry trends and best practices. Attend conferences, join industry associations, and engage in networking opportunities. Surround yourself with like-minded individuals who share your passion for success. By staying connected to the latest developments in your field, you can adapt your strategies and stay ahead of the competition.

In conclusion, applying lessons to your own journey is a critical aspect of entrepreneurship. Seek out mentorship, embrace a growth mindset, and stay informed about industry trends. Remember, your journey is unique, and while learning from successful entrepreneurs can provide valuable insights, it is essential to adapt those lessons to your own circumstances. By doing so, you can pave the way for your own success and achieve your goals as an entrepreneur.

Chapter 15: The Future of Entrepreneurship

Emerging Trends and Opportunities

In today's rapidly evolving business landscape, staying ahead of emerging trends and capitalizing on new opportunities is crucial for start-ups, business owners, and entrepreneurs. The world is constantly changing, and those who adapt and embrace innovation will be in the best position to achieve their goals. This subchapter delves into the emerging trends and opportunities that entrepreneurs should be aware of, providing valuable insights and guidance to navigate this dynamic environment.

One of the most significant emerging trends is the digital transformation. Technology has revolutionized the way we do business, and companies that embrace digital strategies can gain a competitive edge. From e-commerce and online marketing to leveraging data analytics and cloud computing, the opportunities for growth and efficiency are immense. This subchapter explores the various aspects of digital transformation and offers practical advice on how start-ups and business owners can leverage technology to their advantage.

Another trend that entrepreneurs should pay attention to is the rise of social entrepreneurship. In recent years, there has been a growing focus on businesses that prioritize social and environmental impact alongside financial success. Consumers are increasingly conscious of the social and environmental consequences of their purchases, making sustainable and socially responsible businesses more appealing. This subchapter highlights the opportunities in the realm of social entrepreneurship, providing insights on how to integrate purpose-driven initiatives into business models and tap into this emerging market.

Furthermore, the subchapter delves into the importance of innovation and agility. In today's fast-paced world, businesses need to be nimble and adaptable to changes in the market. Start-ups and entrepreneurs need to continuously innovate and seek out new opportunities to stay relevant and seize growth potential. By exploring various innovation frameworks, fostering a culture of creativity, and embracing a growth mindset, entrepreneurs can position themselves to capitalize on emerging trends and opportunities.

Lastly, the subchapter emphasizes the importance of business coaching and mentoring. As entrepreneurs navigate the complex and ever-changing business landscape, having a trusted mentor or coach can make a significant difference. This subchapter provides insights on how to find the right coach or mentor, the benefits of their guidance, and how to make the most of the coaching relationship.

In conclusion, the subchapter on emerging trends and opportunities serves as a valuable resource for start-ups, business owners, and entrepreneurs. By understanding and embracing the digital transformation, exploring social entrepreneurship, fostering innovation and agility, and seeking guidance through coaching and mentoring, entrepreneurs can position themselves for success in today's dynamic business environment.

Adapting to Changing Business Landscape

In today's fast-paced and ever-evolving business world, the ability to adapt to a changing landscape is crucial for the success of any start-up or business. This subchapter explores the importance of adapting to change and provides valuable insights and strategies for entrepreneurs and business owners navigating through uncertain times.

The business landscape is constantly evolving due to technological advancements, market shifts, and changing consumer preferences. As an entrepreneur or business owner, it is essential to recognize the need for adaptability and embrace change as an opportunity for growth. By doing so, you can stay ahead of the competition, seize new opportunities, and ensure the long-term sustainability of your business.

This subchapter delves into the key reasons why adapting to change is crucial in today's business world. It highlights the risks of complacency and the dangers of clinging to outdated practices. Readers will gain a deeper understanding of how embracing change can lead to increased innovation, improved customer satisfaction, and enhanced profitability.

Furthermore, this subchapter provides practical strategies for adapting to a changing business landscape. It explores the importance of continuous learning and staying informed about industry trends. It also emphasizes the significance of fostering a culture of innovation within your organization and regularly reassessing your business model to identify areas for improvement.

For entrepreneurs and business owners seeking guidance in navigating change, this subchapter offers insights into the role of business coaching and mentoring. It explains how engaging with experienced mentors and coaches can provide valuable perspectives, insights, and support during times of transition. Readers will learn how to leverage the expertise of coaches and mentors to overcome challenges, identify opportunities, and develop effective strategies for adapting to change.

In conclusion, "Adapting to Changing Business Landscape" is a crucial subchapter in "The Entrepreneur's Roadmap: Guiding Start-Ups and Business Owners to Achieve their Goals." It offers practical insights and strategies for entrepreneurs and business owners in the niches of business coaching and mentoring. By embracing change and adapting to the evolving business landscape, entrepreneurs can position themselves for long-term success and achieve their goals.

Paving the Way for the Next Generation of Entrepreneurs

In today's rapidly evolving business landscape, it is more important than ever to nurture and support the next generation of entrepreneurs. As start-ups, business owners, and entrepreneurs, we have the unique opportunity to shape the future of our industries and leave a lasting impact on society. This subchapter will explore the significance of paving the way for the next generation of entrepreneurs and provide valuable insights and strategies for business coaching and mentoring.

One of the key reasons why paving the way for the next generation is crucial is the potential for innovation and growth. As seasoned entrepreneurs, we have accumulated a wealth of knowledge and experience that can be shared with aspiring entrepreneurs. By acting as mentors and coaches, we can guide them through the ups and downs of starting and running a business, helping them avoid common pitfalls and accelerating their growth.

Furthermore, supporting the next generation of entrepreneurs is not only beneficial for them but also for the entire business ecosystem. As they bring fresh ideas and perspectives to the table, they have the potential to disrupt industries and drive positive change. By fostering a culture of mentorship and collaboration, we can create a thriving community of entrepreneurs who support and inspire each other, ultimately leading to a more vibrant and innovative business environment.

To effectively pave the way for the next generation, it is essential to adopt a proactive approach to business coaching and mentoring. This involves identifying and nurturing young talent, providing access to resources and networks, and creating opportunities for learning and growth. By sharing our expertise and experiences, we can empower aspiring entrepreneurs to overcome challenges, build resilience, and develop the skills necessary for success.

Additionally, it is important to embrace diversity and inclusivity in our mentoring efforts. By reaching out to individuals from different backgrounds, cultures, and perspectives, we can foster a more inclusive and equitable entrepreneurial ecosystem. This not only ensures that opportunities are available to all but also promotes innovation through the exchange of diverse ideas and viewpoints.

In conclusion, paving the way for the next generation of entrepreneurs is a responsibility that falls on the shoulders of established business owners and entrepreneurs. By actively engaging in business coaching and mentoring, we can empower aspiring entrepreneurs, drive innovation, and create a more inclusive and dynamic business ecosystem. Through our collective efforts, we can shape the future and leave a legacy that inspires generations to come.

Conclusion: Your Roadmap to Success

Recap of Key Takeaways

Throughout this book, "The Entrepreneur's Roadmap: Guiding Start-Ups and Business Owners to Achieve their Goals," we have explored various aspects of entrepreneurship, providing valuable insights and practical advice for start-ups, business owners, and entrepreneurs. In this final subchapter, we will recap the key takeaways from the book, summarizing the most important lessons and reminders for our audience.

1. Embrace the Entrepreneurial Mindset: Success begins with adopting the right mindset. Entrepreneurs must be willing to take risks, be resilient in the face of challenges, and continuously seek opportunities for growth and innovation.

2. Set Clear Goals: Clearly define your business objectives, both short-term and long-term. Setting specific, measurable, achievable, relevant, and time-bound (SMART) goals will help you stay focused and motivated throughout your entrepreneurial journey.

3. Build a Strong Team: Surround yourself with a talented and diverse team that shares your vision and complements your skills. Remember, your team is your most valuable asset, and their collective efforts will drive your business forward.

4. Understand your Target Market: Conduct thorough market research to identify your target audience, their needs, and preferences. This understanding will enable you to develop effective marketing strategies and deliver products or services that truly resonate with your customers.

5. Develop a Robust Business Plan: A well-crafted business plan serves as a roadmap for your entrepreneurial endeavor. It outlines your goals, strategies, financial projections, and potential risks, helping you navigate challenges and seize opportunities.

6. Prioritize Customer Experience: The success of any business relies heavily on customer satisfaction. Focus on delivering exceptional products or services, providing excellent customer service, and establishing strong relationships with your customers.

7. Embrace Continuous Learning: The entrepreneurial journey is a continuous learning process. Stay updated with industry trends, network with like-minded professionals, attend conferences, and invest in your personal and professional growth.

8. Adapt to Change: In today's dynamic business environment, the ability to adapt quickly is crucial. Stay agile, embrace change, and be open to new opportunities that can propel your business forward.

9. Seek Guidance: Consider working with a business coach or mentor who can provide valuable insights, guidance, and support. Their experience and expertise can help you overcome obstacles and achieve your goals more efficiently.

10. Stay Resilient: Entrepreneurship is a rollercoaster ride filled with ups and downs. Stay resilient, learn from failures, and celebrate successes. Remember, perseverance is key to long-term success.

As start-ups, business owners, and entrepreneurs, you have embarked on an exciting and challenging journey. By internalizing these key takeaways and applying them to your own ventures, you are well-equipped to navigate the entrepreneurial landscape and achieve your goals. Remember, success is not achieved overnight, but with passion, dedication, and the right strategies, you can create a thriving business that leaves a lasting impact. Good luck on your entrepreneurial roadmaps!

Encouragement and Motivation for Start-Ups and Business Owners

One of the most critical factors in the success of any start-up or business is the ability to stay motivated and encouraged throughout the entrepreneurial journey. As a start-up founder or business owner, you are bound to face numerous challenges and obstacles along the way. This subchapter aims to provide you with the necessary encouragement and motivation to navigate these hurdles and achieve your goals.

The path of entrepreneurship can be a lonely one, filled with uncertainty and self-doubt. However, it is essential to remember that you are not alone in this journey. Many successful entrepreneurs have faced similar challenges and overcome them to build thriving businesses. By understanding their stories and learning from their experiences, you can find inspiration in their success.

Surrounding yourself with positive and like-minded individuals is another key aspect of staying motivated. Seeking out a business coach or mentor who specializes in your niche can provide you with valuable guidance and support. These individuals have often been through the same challenges you are facing and can offer practical advice, encouragement, and accountability to keep you on track.

In addition to seeking external support, it is crucial to cultivate a strong internal motivation. This can be achieved by setting clear and achievable goals for your business. By breaking down your long-term objectives into smaller, manageable milestones, you can celebrate each accomplishment and maintain a sense of progress. Regularly reviewing and adjusting your goals will help you stay focused and motivated.

Another effective strategy for staying motivated is to celebrate your successes, no matter how small they may seem. Acknowledging your achievements boosts your confidence and provides a source of motivation during challenging times. Remember that every setback is an opportunity for growth and learning, so embrace failure as a stepping stone towards success.

Finally, taking care of your overall well-being is crucial for maintaining motivation. Entrepreneurship can be mentally and physically demanding, so it is essential to prioritize self-care. Engaging in activities such as exercise, meditation, or hobbies can help alleviate stress and rejuvenate your mind.

In conclusion, staying motivated and encouraged throughout your entrepreneurial journey is vital for the success of your start-up or business. By seeking inspiration from successful entrepreneurs, surrounding yourself with support, setting clear goals, celebrating achievements, embracing failure, and prioritizing self-care, you can stay motivated and overcome any obstacle that comes your way. Remember, you have what it takes to achieve your goals and build a thriving business. Keep pushing forward, and success will follow.

Final Words of Advice for Achieving Goals

Congratulations! You have embarked on an exciting journey as a start-up, business owner, or entrepreneur. The path you have chosen is full of challenges and uncertainties, but also opportunities for growth and success. As you navigate through this entrepreneurial road, we would like to offer you some final words of advice that will help you achieve your goals.

1. Stay Focused: One of the key elements of achieving your goals is to maintain laser-like focus. It is easy to get distracted by the myriad of tasks and opportunities that come your way. Remember to stay true to your vision and prioritize tasks that align with your long-term objectives. By staying focused, you will be able to make progress consistently and efficiently.

2. Set SMART Goals: To achieve your goals, it is important to set SMART goals – Specific, Measurable, Achievable, Relevant, and Time-bound. Break down your bigger goals into smaller, manageable milestones. This will help you track your progress and stay motivated as you achieve each milestone along the way.

3. Seek Guidance: As an entrepreneur, it is crucial to seek guidance from experienced business coaches and mentors. They can provide you with valuable insights, share their own experiences, and offer guidance on overcoming obstacles. Surround yourself with a network of like-minded individuals who can offer support and guidance as you navigate the challenges of entrepreneurship.

4. Embrace Failure: Failure is an inevitable part of the entrepreneurial journey. Instead of being discouraged by it, embrace failure as an opportunity to learn and grow. Analyze what went wrong, make adjustments, and keep moving forward. Remember, every setback is an opportunity for a comeback.

5. Stay Agile: The business landscape is constantly evolving, and as an entrepreneur, you need to stay agile. Be open to change and adapt your strategies as needed. Keep a keen eye on market trends, customer needs, and emerging technologies. By staying agile, you will be able to seize new opportunities and stay ahead of the competition.

6. Celebrate Successes: Finally, don't forget to celebrate your successes, no matter how small they may seem. Recognize and reward yourself and your team for achieving milestones and reaching goals. Celebrating successes will not only boost morale but also inspire you to keep pushing forward towards bigger and more ambitious goals.

In conclusion, achieving your goals as a start-up, business owner, or entrepreneur requires focus, strategic planning, resilience, and the support of a strong network. By staying focused, setting SMART goals, seeking guidance, embracing failure, staying agile, and celebrating successes, you will be well on your way to achieving your entrepreneurial dreams. Remember, every step taken towards your goals is a step closer to success. Good luck on your entrepreneurial journey!

Printed in Great Britain
by Amazon

41167086R00056